The Hubble Space Telescope

Margaret W. Carruthers

Franklin Watts
A Division of Scholastic Inc.
New York • Toronto • London • Auckland • Sydney
Mexico City • New Delhi • Hong Kong
Danbury, Connecticut

For Storm

Special thanks to Dorothy Fraquelli at the Space Telescope Science Institute for her constructive review of the manuscript.

Note to readers: Definitions for words in **bold** can be found in the Glossary at the back of this book.

Photographs ©2003:Corbis Images: 10 (Bettmann), 8 (Simon Fraser/SPL); Corbis Sygma/Jeffrey Markowitz: 15; NASA: 42 top (H. Ford-JHU, G. Illingworth-USCS/LO, M. Clampin, G. Hartig-STScI, ACS Team), 38 bottom left (Kitt Peak National Observatory/NOAO/M. Bolte-U. of California, Santa Cruz), 39 left (Dr. Christopher Burrows/ESA/STScI), 20 (Andrea Dupree-Harvard-Smithsonian CfA, Ronald Gilliland-STScI/ESA), 39 top (J.J. Hester-Arizona State University), 44 (R. Williams-STScI/Hubble Deep Field Team), 38 top, 42 bottom, 43 (Hubble Heritage Team/STScI/AURA), 37 (Hubble Space Telescope Comet Team), 36 (Phil James-Univ. Toledo, Todd Clancy-SSI, Boulder, Steve Lee-Univ. Colorado), 16 (D. Maoz-Tel-Aviv University and Columbia University/ESA), 38 bottom right (Harvey Richer-U. of British Columbia, Vancouver), 27 (R. Saffer-Villanova University), 3 right, 34 (STScI/AURA), 7 (J. Trauger), 39 bottom right (Fred Walter-State University of New York at Stony Brook), 13; Northrop Grumman Corporation: 46; Photo Researchers, NY/Space Telescope Science Institute/SPL: 26; Photri Inc./NASA: 4, 14, 22, 32; Visuals Unlimited: 24 (Jeff J. Daly), cover, 3 left, 30 (Science/NASA).

Library of Congress Cataloging-in-Publication Data

Carruthers, Margaret W.
    The Hubble Space Telescope / Margaret W. Carruthers.
        p. cm. — (Watts library)
    Summary: A comprehensive look at the Hubble Space Telescope which has, since 1990, collected information about our solar system, star clusters in the Milky Way galaxy, and even other galaxies as it orbits the Earth.
    Includes bibliographical references and index.
    ISBN 0-531-12279-4 (lib. bdg.)   0-531-16372-5 (pbk.)
    1. Hubble Space Telescope (Spacecraft)—Juvenile literature. [1. Hubble Space Telescope (Spacecraft) 2. Telescopes. 3. Outer space—Exploration.] I. Title. II. Series.
QB500.268.C37 2003
522'.29'19—dc21
                                                                    2003005816

Contents

Its instruments trained on more distant vistas, in this artist's conception, the Hubble Space Telescope orbits in space above the continent of Africa and the Arabian Peninsula.

Chapter One

A New Eye on the Universe

Orbiting 375 miles (600 kilometers) above Earth's surface is an eye that can see to the edge of the known universe. It has watched the icy shards of a comet smash into the churning atmosphere of a giant **planet**. It has peered deep into the nurseries of newborn stars. It has witnessed **galaxies** colliding and glimpsed giant stars exploding.

Since 1990 this eye, better known as the Hubble Space Telescope, has been collecting light from objects in our **solar system**, from stars in our Milky Way galaxy, and from galaxies billions of light-years away. The information it gathers helps scientists better understand what giant planets are made of, how stars form, and what lies at the hearts of swirling galaxies. It lets us test theories and form new ideas about how things work in the universe. Scientists hope that, ultimately, the Hubble Space Telescope will help us answer questions such as: How big is the universe? How old is it? How did it form? Why does it look the way it does? Is there anyone else out there?

How a Telescope Got to Space

In 1609, an Italian **astronomer** named Galileo Galilei (1564-1642) peered into the night sky through a couple of pieces of glass mounted inside a tube. The two pieces of glass, called lenses, worked together to magnify and focus the light coming through the tube. As a result, the instrument made things look three times closer than usual, and it allowed Galileo to see much farther than he could with just his eyes. This new, high-tech piece of scientific equipment was called the **telescope**.

Galileo didn't invent the telescope, but he was one of the first scientists to use it. Over the years he made more and more powerful telescopes. With them he studied objects no one had ever been able to see before, things like craters on the Moon, the four large moons of Jupiter, and the stars that make up the Milky Way. For nearly four hundred years, people have been modifying and improving telescopes so they can help us see

As shown here, Hubble enabled scientists to view images of individual stars within the whirling spiral arms of spiral galaxy M100. From ground-based telescopes on Earth, such stars appear blurred together, making it difficult for scientists to accurately measure their light.

things that are smaller, dimmer, and farther away. Astronomers have used telescopes to discover planets, map and track stars, and figure out the shape of the Milky Way and other galaxies. But telescopes on the ground have always had one big problem: air.

The Problem with the Atmosphere

Soon after the telescope was invented, astronomers noticed that the atmosphere was getting in the way of their views of the stars and planets. Earth's atmosphere is made of molecules of chemicals such as nitrogen, oxygen, water, and carbon dioxide.

Many large ground-based telescopes, such as Kek I and Kek II on the top of Mauna Kea in Hawaii, are placed on mountaintops. This reduces the amount of atmosphere between the telescopes and the stars they are observing.

These molecules scatter the light coming in from space, making the stars and planets appear fuzzy. (The same thing happens on the ground on a foggy day: water droplets in the fog reflect and distort the light so we can't see things clearly.) To make things worse, air molecules also soak up, or absorb, light. Some forms of light never make it to a telescope at all.

Astronomers tried to overcome these problems by making observations from mountaintops. At high elevations the air is thinner—there are fewer air molecules to scatter and absorb the light. This helped, but even mountaintops have plenty of air, so it didn't completely solve the problem.

In 1923, a rocket scientist named Hermann Oberth from what is now Romania came up with a solution: why not put a telescope in orbit around Earth? That way it could look out into space, gathering light from distant stars while high above the atmosphere. The problem at the time was that no one had ever sent *anything* into space, much less a complicated scientific instrument. Scientists and engineers would have to figure out how to launch something into space, how to keep it in orbit around Earth, and how to communicate with it. After all, a space telescope wouldn't be of much use if it couldn't send information back to Earth.

Thirty-four years later, engineers had most of the problems cracked. In October 1957, the Soviet Union launched *Sputnik 1*, Earth's first artificial **satellite**, into orbit and the space age began. Three months later, the United States put its first satellite, *Explorer 1*, in orbit. The United States was very serious about its space program, and in 1958 it created NASA, the National Aeronautics and Space Administration.

Scientists and engineers wanted NASA to do a lot of things—keep up with the Soviets, explore the planets, and send a man to the Moon. Eventually, they also wanted a space telescope that could explore places farther away than any human or spacecraft could ever go.

The very first orbiting space observatory was launched in April 1962. Great Britain and the United States worked together to send *Ariel 1* into orbit to study **ultraviolet lights** and X rays from the Sun. Since neither of these types of light is visible from Earth (the atmosphere absorbs them), *Ariel 1* gave scientists a different look at the Sun. Then in 1968, NASA launched the orbiting telescope *OAO-II*. For four and a half years, it looked at the ultraviolet light coming from galaxies, stars, planets, and comets.

Over the next few years, different countries launched several more space observatories. Although they were all useful, allowing astronomers to see things they'd never seen before, none was as big and powerful as the giant space telescope they'd dreamed about.

The scientist for whom the Hubble Space Telescope is named, Dr. Edwin Hubble, looks through the Schmidt telescope at the Palomar Observatory in California.

The OK from Congress

In 1977, the United States Congress agreed to give NASA the money it needed to construct an enormous and extremely advanced space telescope. NASA hired engineers to help design and build the telescope. It formed the Space Telescope Science Institute (STScI) to deal with all the information the telescope would send back to Earth. And finally, NASA named the new space telescope Hubble, after the American astronomer Edwin Hubble.

Edwin Hubble, the Expanding Universe, and the Big Bang Theory

Edwin Powell Hubble (1889-1953) was one of the most important astronomers of the twentieth century. Ever since

Optical Telescopes

The Hubble Space Telescope is a type of **optical telescope**. Optical telescopes gather visible light from space. (Other kinds of telescopes, such as **radio telescopes** and x-ray telescopes, observe different forms, or **wavelengths**, of light.)

There are two kinds of optical telescopes: **refracting telescopes** and **reflecting telescopes**. Both are designed to gather light from space and focus it into a sharp image, but they do it in different ways. Refracting telescopes focus the light using clear glass lenses (like eyeglasses). When the light moves from the air to the lens, it bends, or refracts. Galileo's telescopes were refracting telescopes. Reflecting telescopes, on the other hand, use curved mirrors to focus the light. When light enters the telescope, it bounces, or reflects, off the mirrors to the viewer. Hubble Space Telescope is a reflecting telescope.

Galileo looked at the Milky Way through his telescope in the 1600s, people have known that it is made of many millions of stars. But before the 1920s, no one was sure whether or not the Milky Way was the *only* galaxy in the universe. They could see clouds of something out there (the misty regions were named **nebulae**, the Latin word for "clouds"), but they weren't sure what the nebulae were made of.

Using the telescope at the Mount Wilson Observatory in Southern California, Edwin Hubble looked closely at the Andromeda nebula. In 1924, he discovered that the Nebula is actually composed of millions of stars, just like the Milky Way. The Andromeda nebula is now called the Andromeda Galaxy. Astronomers would eventually find that the universe contains thousands of millions of other galaxies as well.

In 1929, Hubble made another extraordinary discovery. He observed that other galaxies are moving away from us, and that the farther away a galaxy is, the faster it is moving. This means that everything in the universe is moving away from everything else. In other words, *the universe is expanding*.

This discovery was important not just because it helped us understand what is happening in the universe today. It also gave scientists some ideas about how the universe formed in the first place. If the universe is expanding, then it must have been smaller in the past. If it has always been expanding, then when it first formed, it must have been infinitely small. Most astronomers now think that the universe formed from an enormous explosion known as the Big Bang.

A Tragic Delay

HST was originally scheduled to be launched in February 1986. But in January, the space shuttle *Challenger* exploded less than two minutes after takeoff, killing everyone on board. All new projects were put on hold.

Hubble is a particularly good name for the space telescope because it has expanded our view of the universe.

HST Is Launched

Thirteen years after the plans began, 67 years after the idea of a space telescope was first published, and 382 years after the telescope was invented, the Hubble Space Telescope (or **HST** for short) was ready to go.

On April 24, 1990, HST lifted off from the Kennedy Space Center in Florida, aboard the space shuttle *Discovery*. The next day, shuttle astronauts 600 km (375 miles) over the Andes Mountains of South America took Hubble out of the cargo bay and shoved it out into space. Hubble was on its own, orbiting Earth at 17,500 miles per hour (28,000 km per hour).

Watched by its sister ship, the space shuttle Columbia *(left), the space shuttle* Discovery *lifts off (right) carrying a most precious cargo: the Hubble Space Telescope.*

A crew member on the space shuttle Endeavour *took this picture of HST at the completion of the shuttle's mission to repair the telescope.*

Calling in the Repair Crew

With Hubble finally in orbit, astronomers were eager to see the exotic images it would send back. But scientists noticed a problem almost immediately. The images weren't as clear as they should have been. It turned out that the telescope's main mirror wasn't exactly the right shape. Mirrors are used

to collect light from space and focus it into a clear image. If a mirror isn't made perfectly, it doesn't focus the light correctly and the images are fuzzy.

Fortunately, not every instrument on HST needs a perfect mirror. Astronomers were still able to do things such as measure star brightness and calculate how fast galaxies are moving. But not having clear pictures was a big disappointment, especially to the public who had been promised that HST would send back the most extraordinary images of the universe anyone had ever seen.

So for the next three and a half years, scientists, designers, engineers, and astronauts worked on a solution. In December 1993, astronauts aboard the space shuttle *Endeavor* made the first Hubble servicing mission, basically a telescope tune-up. Their main task was to install Hubble's new contact lenses: the COSTAR corrective optics package. COSTAR allowed the telescope to see properly. Since the end of 1993, the telescope has been collecting clear, beautiful pictures of the universe.

These two images of the same star show HST's capabilities before (left) and after (right) the repair mission in late 1993.

This is a composite HST image of spiral galaxy NGC 1512, showing the galaxy at all wavelengths of light, from ultraviolet to infrared. At the center of the galaxy is a huge circle of infant star clusters, known to scientists as a starburst ring.

Chapter Two

How the Hubble Works

The Hubble Space Telescope is 43.5 feet long (13.2 meters) and about 14 feet (4m) across—about the size of a tractor trailer or a school bus. It has a **mass** of 11,000 kilograms, which means that it weighs about 24,000 pounds on Earth. It is made of 100,000 different parts, which control the telescope, provide power, gather and analyze light from space, and communicate with scientists and engineers on the ground.

Keeping on Target

If you've ever tried to focus on something with a camera, you know how difficult it can be to keep your hand steady, even for just a second. Imagine trying to focus on something millions of light-years away, while speeding around Earth at 17,500 miles per hour (28,000 km/h). Imagine doing it for a few hours.

Hubble must often focus on an object for several hours in order to collect enough light. To keep pointed in the right direction, Hubble has a sophisticated Pointing Control System, or PCS. The PCS is a group of instruments that work together to steer and point Hubble. A few of the sensors lock onto particular stars called guide stars. This is like keeping a landmark such as a tall building or a particular mountain peak in view so you always have some idea as to where you are. Other sensors note Hubble's orientation to the Sun, figure out where Hubble is in relation to Earth's magnetic field, and keep

Measuring Space

How big an object looks in the sky depends on both its true size and how far away it is. One way astronomers describe things is by how much of the sky they take up. Astronomers measure distances across the sky in degrees, minutes, and seconds, rather than miles, feet, and inches. There are 60 minutes in 1 degree, and 60 seconds in 1 minute. Something that completely encircled Earth would be 360 degrees of arc, or 1,296,000 seconds of arc (arcseconds). The Moon is about 0.5° (30 minutes, or 1,800 arcseconds) across. The Hubble Space Telescope can see things that are so small or so far away that they are less than 0.1 arcseconds across.

track of all its movements. Meanwhile, another group of instruments responds to the information the sensors gather, adjusting Hubble to keep it in the right position and focused on the object it is studying.

Gathering Light

As light travels through space, it spreads out in the same way that light from a flashlight spreads out. The farther it travels, the more it spreads. The farther you are from a light source like a star, the less light gets to you. That's why it can be so difficult to see things that are very far away. HST deals with this problem in several ways. First of all, it has a large primary mirror. The bigger the mirror, the more light it can gather at once and the farther it can see. Secondly, it can stay steady so it can look at one target for a long time and collect light for a long time. Finally, the telescope's electronic eyes are a lot more sensitive to light than our eyes are.

Once the telescope is pointed at the right target, it can start gathering light. Say the telescope is pointed at Betelgeuse. Betelgeuse is a bright, **red supergiant** star in the constellation Orion. Betelgeuse is fairly close, only 600 light-years from Earth. This means that it takes 600 years for the light from Betelgeuse to get to us. So what we see in the night sky, and what HST sees, is what Betelgeuse looked like 600 years ago.

When the starlight gets to the telescope, it travels through a long tube that shields the telescope from the glare of the Sun and Earth. Inside the tube are two mirrors: a large primary

At left is the HST image of the star Betelgeuse, which is highlighted at right as the "shoulder" in the constellation Orion the Hunter. The glow at the center of Betelgeuse has puzzled scientists so far; what they do know is that the bright spot is 10 times wider than the diameter of Earth.

Size of Star

Size of Earth's Orbit

Size of Jupiter's Orbit

Atmosphere of Betelgeuse · Alpha Orionis
Hubble Space Telescope · Faint Object Camera

PRC96-04 · ST ScI OPO · January 15, 1996 · A. Dupree (CfA), NASA, ESA

mirror, which is about 8 ft (2.4m) across, and a smaller secondary mirror. The two mirrors face each other.

The light from Betelgeuse hits the primary mirror and bounces off. It then hits the secondary mirror and reflects back towards the primary mirror. Both of the mirrors are curved. If they were flat, they would reflect light straight back. But because they're curved, the light gets focused into a beam. The light then travels through a hole drilled in the center of the primary mirror. Behind that hole are the eyes of the telescope.

Backyard telescopes work pretty much the same way. Light from space travels through a tube, reflects off two mirrors, and then travels to your eyes. But there are no astronomers floating in space, looking through HST. Instead, Hubble has electronic eyes. Cameras and **spectrographs** collect the light from space and record it so that scientists on the ground can look at it whenever they want.

Different Cameras for Different Things

Hubble has a number of different cameras and other instruments. Some are designed to look at a large area of the sky, maybe hundreds of galaxies at once. Others are made to look closely at one small target, such as a distant star. Some sense visible forms of light, which we can see with our eyes, while others detect infrared or ultraviolet light, which humans can't

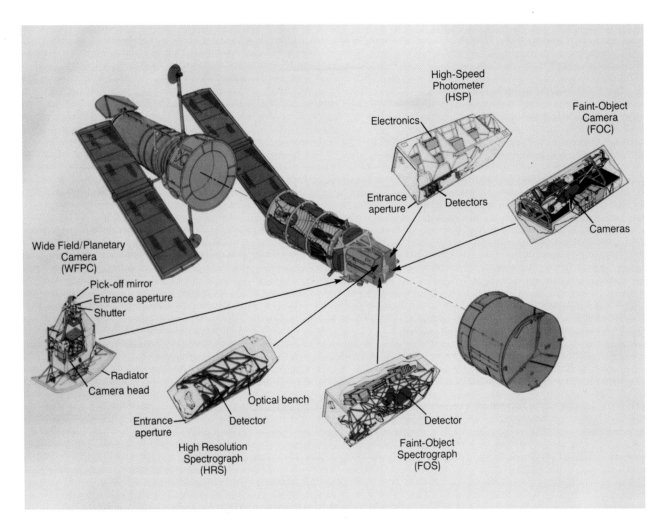

High-Speed
Photometer
(HSP)

Electronics

Faint-Object
Camera
(FOC)

Entrance
aperture

Detectors

Cameras

Wide Field/Planetary
Camera
(WFPC)

Pick-off mirror

Entrance aperture

Shutter

Radiator

Camera head

Entrance
aperture

Optical bench

Detector

Detector

Faint-Object
Spectrograph
(FOS)

High Resolution
Spectrograph
(HRS)

The HST's observations are actually conducted by five different scientific instruments. The five instruments shown in this diagram were on HST when it was launched in 1990.

see. Some instruments look at all the light at once, and others separate the light into different wavelengths.

All of Hubble's cameras are digital cameras. This means that they don't have film in them like regular cameras. Instead, they have electronic detectors that can sense every photon, or piece of light, that hits them. These electronic detectors are much more sensitive than film, so they can record light from very dim objects.

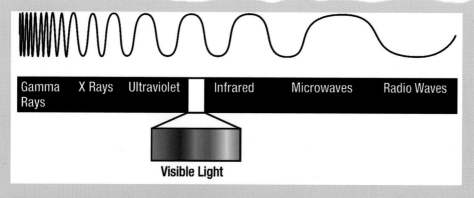

Electromagnetic Radiation

Visible light is a type of electromagnetic radiation. Radio waves, microwaves, infrared light, ultraviolet light, X rays, and gamma rays are other types. Electromagnetic radiation travels as waves (similar to water waves). Each type has a different wavelength, the distance between two peaks on the wave. Radio waves are very long, while gamma rays are very short. Visible light waves are in between, and each color of visible light has a different wavelength. Violet and blue have shorter wavelengths than red and orange. Green and yellow are in between. The range of light, from gamma rays to radio waves, is called the **electromagnetic spectrum**.

The other advantage of digital cameras is that the images can be stored on a computer and beamed back to Earth almost as soon as they're taken. If HST used film cameras, we would have to send astronauts up to change the film. Scientists would have to wait months for their photographs to be developed.

Spectrographs

Although sunlight looks white to us, it is actually made of all of the colors of the rainbow: red, orange, yellow, green, blue, indigo, and violet. English physicist Isaac Newton (1642-

Sunlight is broken into the colors of the visible spectrum by this triangular prism.

1727) first discovered this when he watched rays of light travel through a glass prism. When the white light came out of the other side of the prism, it had been transformed into bands of different colors.

This happens because light bends when it travels from one material into another. Each color of light bends a different amount. So when the light passes from the air into the glass and back out into the air again, the colors separate enough that we can see them individually. (Rainbows occur for the same reason: light separates into different colors when it passes through water droplets.)

So we know that although sunlight looks white, it is made of many different colors. This is true for the light of other stars as well. A star might look very red, but it actually has some yellow, orange, green, and blue in it as well. It is also true for light that reflects off objects such as planets. Planets give off no light of their own. The light we see from planets is actually reflected starlight.

The range of colors that a star emits is called its spectrum (spectra is the plural). To study a star's spectrum, astronomers can use an instrument called a spectrograph. The spectrograph is like a prism with a camera attached: it spreads the light into its different colors, allowing scientists to measure the amount of each color.

You might wonder why anyone would go to the trouble of finding out exactly what colors a star truly is. The reason is that the colors provide information. Think about what colors

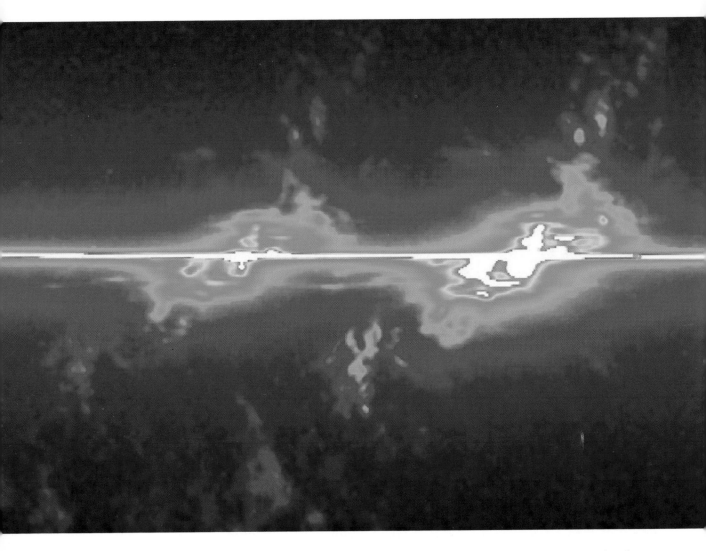

The HST spectrograph image shows gases streaming from the nucleus of the Seyfert Galaxy, NGC 4151. Scientists think that a massive black hole lies at the heart of NGC 4151.

tell us in everyday life. We can tell how healthy grass is by how green it is, or estimate how old a metal fence is by examining the amount of reddish-brown rust on it. The color of a planet helps us figure out what its surface is made of and what gases are in its atmosphere. The color of starlight can tell us how hot the star is, how old it is, what it's made of, how fast it's going, and what direction it's heading.

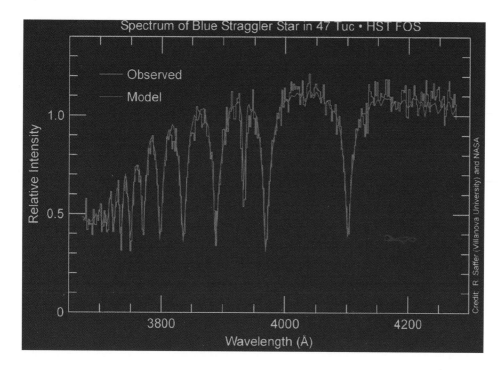

Spectrum of Blue Straggler Star in 47 Tuc • HST FOS

Credit: R. Saffer (Villanova University) and NASA

Scientists can use a star's light to learn things about it that an image alone will not reveal. Here, scientists have used data captured by Hubble to chart the spectrum of light from an object known as a blue straggler star.

Relaying Starlight

After the light from Betelgeuse travels for 600 years towards Earth, goes into the telescope, bounces off the mirrors, and hits the cameras and spectrographs, it must somehow get to scientists on the ground. Actually, the light itself doesn't need to get to the ground, but information about it does.

HST records the information in its onboard computers and then sends it to a relay satellite. A few different relay satellites are part of the Tracking and Data Relay Satellite System (TDRSS). Unlike Hubble, which circles Earth every ninety-seven minutes, these satellites are in geosynchronous orbit thousands of miles high. This means that they orbit at the same rate as Earth rotates, so they hover above a single point

Scientific Instruments on the Hubble Space Telescope

Instrument Name	Abbreviation	Purpose	Date Installed	Date Removed
High Speed Photometer	HSP	to measure changes in brightness of various objects	April 1990	December 1993
Wide Field / Planetary Camera 1	WF/PC 1	works in two modes: wide field mode to see large areas, and planetary mode to look more closely at nearby targets like planets and comets	April 1990	December 1993
Goddard High Resolution Spectrograph	GHRS	to observe the ultraviolet spectra of bright targets such as nearby stars	April 1990	December 1997
Faint Object Spectrograph	FOS	to look at the spectra of targets far away	April 1990	December 1997
Faint Object Camera 1	FOC	to look at very faint targets far away	April 1990	March 2002
Wide Field / Planetary Camera 2	WF/PC 2	updated version of WF/PC 1	December 1993	scheduled for 2004
Corrective Optics Space Telescope Axial Replacement	COSTAR	a system of mirrors used to refocus light to make up for the flaw in HST's main mirror	December 1993	scheduled for 2004 (out of use since 2002)
Space Telescope Imaging Spectrograph	STIS	to record the spectra of various objects	February 1997	scheduled for 2010

Near Infrared Camera / Multi-Object Spectrometer	NICMOS	to look at infrared light	February 1997	scheduled for 2010
Advanced Camera for Surveys	ACS	to survey large regions of space	February 2002	scheduled for 2010
Cosmic Origins Spectrograph	COS	to observe ultraviolet spectra of faint targets	scheduled for 2004	scheduled for 2010
Wide Field / Planetary Camera 3	WF/PC 3	to replace WF/PC 2	scheduled for 2004	scheduled for 2010

on Earth. Since they don't move relative to anything on the ground, engineers can keep in contact with them almost continuously.

After the relay satellite gathers the data from Hubble, it sends the data to the White Sands Antennae Array in New Mexico. The array consists of a bunch of satellite dishes, each 60 feet (20m) across. Then the information gets passed on to the Space Telescope Operations Control Center (STOCC for short) at the Goddard Space Flight Center in Greenbelt, Maryland. Finally, STOCC sends the data on to the Space Telescope Science Institute (STScI) in Baltimore, Maryland.

When engineers want the telescope to do something, the commands go the other way. From Greenbelt, they travel to White Sands. White Sands sends the commands to the relay satellites, which then send them on to the telescope. It takes about a minute for a command to get to the telescope from the control center.

When information from HST gets to Baltimore, scientists at STScI convert it back into images. The scientists who want to study those images can then go to STScI, have STScI send them the images on cd-rom, or download them via the Internet.

Upgrading

The HST is redeployed after being successfully repaired by a specially trained crew from the space shuttle.

It takes a long time to design a spacecraft. By the time it gets launched, the scientific instruments and computers are a bit out of date. After a few years, they are *way* out of date. The *Voyager 1* spacecraft, for example, which was launched in 1977 and is now on its way out of the solar system, has a computer

that is nowhere near as good as the cheapest laptop for sale today.

Engineers were aware of this problem while they were designing Hubble. They also knew that if the telescope had any problems or just needed some routine maintenance, it would be extremely expensive, if not impossible, to bring it back to Earth to fix. So they designed HST so that it could be serviced, repaired, and upgraded by astronauts while in orbit. As of 2003, the telescope has been tuned up five times. The instruments it now has on board are much better than the ones it started out with.

Staying in Orbit

Like any other satellite (including the Moon), HST orbits Earth. It circles the planet without falling to the ground or flying out into space. HST stays in orbit because the force that pulls it towards Earth is balanced by the force that pushes it out into space.

The force that pulls HST towards Earth is gravity. Gravity is a force of attraction between two objects. Its strength depends on how **massive** the two objects are and how close they are. The more massive the objects, the stronger the gravitational attraction. And the closer they are, the stronger the attraction. The gravitational attraction between HST and Earth is fairly strong because Earth is very massive and the two objects are quite close.

Tools in Space

The Pistol Grip Tool, or PGT for short, was the first cordless power tool in space. Astronauts used it to work on Hubble in 1997 and in 1999.

Six hundred kilometers above Bolivia, Chile, and Peru, the Hubble Space Telescope (HST) begins to separate from the arm of the remote manipulator system of the space shuttle Discovery. *HST had just been released by the shuttle into its own orbit.*

Giving Hubble a Boost

Although HST orbits about 375 miles (600 km) above the surface of Earth, it is still traveling through its atmosphere. This part of the atmosphere is very, very thin, but there are enough air molecules to get in the way and slow Hubble down. As a result, Hubble slowly loses altitude, falling into even thicker atmosphere, which slows it down even more. This process is called orbital decay. If nothing were done, Hubble would eventually fall back to Earth. To keep this from happening, every so often space shuttle astronauts give the telescope a reboost to move it into a higher orbit.

The force that pushes HST out into space is related to its velocity, the speed and direction it is going. Unless some other force acts on it, an object's velocity will stay the same forever. Once you give it a little push, it will keep on going. This does not happen down on Earth because there are a lot of other forces that get in the way. If you roll a ball down a straight flat street, it will eventually come to a stop. Friction with the ground slows it down, while the air molecules in the atmosphere get in the way to slow it down even more. But out in space, there isn't much to get in the way. HST got its velocity of 17,500 miles per hour (28,000 km/h) from traveling aboard the space shuttle *Discovery*, which was propelled by burning rocket fuel.

HST images such as this one, of galaxy NGC 3310, have enabled scientists to study a phenomenon known as starburst galaxies, which are galaxies where stars are being formed at an unusually fast rate.

Chapter Three

Hubble's Universe

As of 2003, Hubble has looked closely at more than 50,000 points in space. Scientists have studied the data and written more than 4,000 reports about it. Every day, HST gathers about four gigabytes of data—enough to fill an entire set of encyclopedias. If it were printed, this data would fill half the Library of Congress. Obviously, it would be impossible to write about everything we've learned from Hubble in one book. So here are just a few of Hubble's "Greatest Hits."

Our Solar System

To get a really good look at a planet, we have to send a spacecraft into orbit around it or even land a spacecraft on the surface. As good as HST is, it can't actually see planets up close. It can't see the details that spacecraft like *Magellan*, which went to Venus, or *Galileo*, which went to Jupiter, have shown us. But what Hubble can do is look at a planet more frequently, at short notice, or when no probe is there. It is especially useful for studying things that happen quickly, such as weather changes and comet impacts.

By creating a mosaic of many different images taken by the HST, scientists have been able to measure and observe the extent of the change by seasons in the ice cap at the North Pole of the planet Mars.

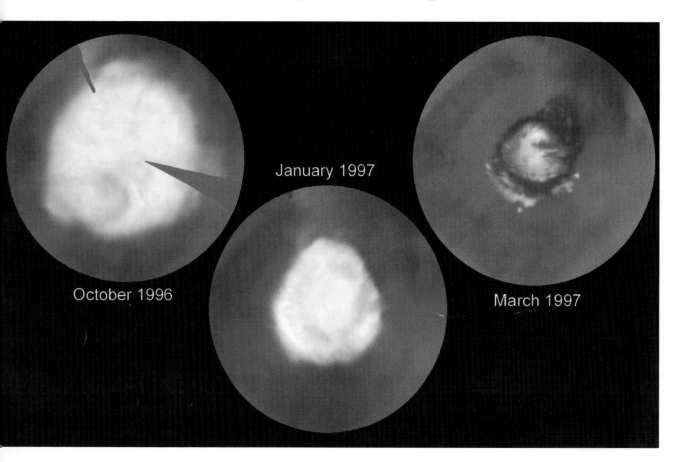

October 1996

January 1997

March 1997

In July 1994, Comet Shoemaker-Levy 9 crashed into Jupiter, leaving scars the size of Earth.

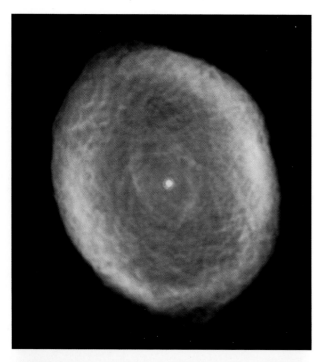

This is a Hubble image of the object known as the planetary nebula IC 418, which lies about 2,000 light-years from Earth near the constellation Lepus. A planetary nebula is the final stage in the evolution of a star similar to our Sun. Our Sun will reach a stage similar to this some day—about 5 billion years from now!

Below, at left is an HST image of **white dwarf** stars in the globular cluster M4, which, at a distance of 7,000 light-years away, is the closest such cluster to Earth. At right is an HST image of a smaller portion of M4. The objects circled in blue are white dwarfs.

Ground

HST

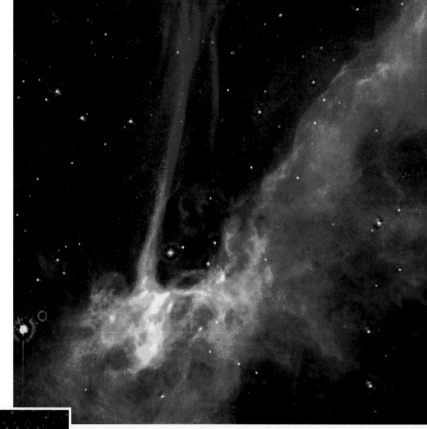

Hubble captured this striking image of what is known as the Cygnus Loop **supernova** *remnant. The Cygnus Loop is the edge of an expanding blast wave from the huge explosion of a star some 15,000 years ago.*

In February 1994, Hubble captured this image of three rings of glowing gas surrounding supernova 1987A, a star that exploded in 1987. The supernova is 169,000 light years away in the dwarf galaxy known as the Large Magellanic Cloud.

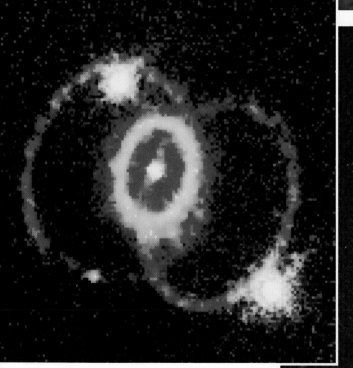

Hubble has provided scientists and casual viewers alike with their first views of many objects in space. In this case, it is a lone neutron star (marked with arrow). From this image, scientists were able to determine the star's temperature and size. Scientists know that an object this small, hot, and dim must be a neutron star.

The Lives of Stars

If biologists want to study the life cycle of a frog, they can simply watch frog eggs develop into tadpoles and then into frogs. It happens so quickly that a biologist can observe many generations of frogs and become a real expert in the way that frogs develop.

The same is not true for astronomers studying the life cycle of stars. Stars take a very long time to evolve, much longer than a human lifetime. Even the most massive stars, which have the shortest life spans, take thousands of years to form and then burn for millions of years more.

One way to figure out how stars evolve is to use what we already know about physics and chemistry. If scientists know what a star is made of, they can calculate or predict how it should evolve over time.

Another way to gain information about stars is to take thousands of images of thousands of different stars. If we took hundreds of photographs of pond life, we would end up with pictures of frog eggs, hatching eggs, tadpoles, tadpoles with legs, young frogs, adult frogs, frogs laying eggs, old frogs, and dying frogs. Even if we never saw a single frog egg develop into an adult frog, we could figure out how frogs develop from the photographs.

Similarly, if we take enough pictures of enough stars, we should end up with images of all different kinds of stars at all different stages of evolution. The Hubble Space Telescope is the perfect instrument for this job.

Galaxies

Ever since Edwin Hubble discovered the nature of the Andromeda Galaxy in 1924, astronomers have been fascinated with the variety of galaxies beyond the Milky Way. With HST, astronomers can now investigate thousands of different galaxies. They can use Hubble to figure out what galaxies are made of, how old they are, how they form and evolve, and why they look the way they do.

The Edge of the Universe

Some parts of the sky look completely black. Even with a telescope, you can't see anything. Are these black parts of the sky actually empty parts of space, or is there light coming from them that is just too dim to see?

In 1995, scientists tried to answer this question by pointing HST at a spot near the handle of the Big Dipper where no light had ever been observed. They knew that to catch a glimpse of anything that might be there, Hubble's eye would have to stay open for a long time. The longer HST looked, the better the image would be. So for ten days and nights, while going around Earth 150 times, HST shot photo after photo of the same dark part of the sky.

When astronomers combined all 342 pictures, they came up with one of Hubble's most famous and most exciting images: the Hubble Deep Field.

The Hubble Deep Field covers a patch of sky that is only one-thirtieth of the diameter of the full Moon. Although it

Opposite, top: In April 2002, Hubble's newly installed Advance Camera for Surveys provided this image of the collision and merger of two galaxies nicknamed by scientists "the Mice" for their shape and long, thin "tails."

Opposite, bottom: Galaxy ESO 510-G13 looks so thin because we are seeing it from the side.

An HST image of the whirlpool galaxy M51. If nothing else, Hubble reveals how complexly beautiful the universe is.

The Hubble Deep Field was one of HST's most important, and most famous, images. It revealed galaxies that formed less than one billion years after the Big Bang.

looks black and empty from Earth, it actually contains more than 1,500 galaxies. The Hubble Deep Field has galaxy shapes no one had ever seen before, and stars four billion times fainter than the human eye can see.

It might seem that all of the objects in the Hubble Deep Field are all the same distance from Earth. In fact, the objects in the Hubble Deep Field are at various distances from Earth. In general, the closer they are, the brighter and bigger they look. The farther they are, the smaller and dimmer. Looking at the Hubble Deep Field is like peering down a tunnel towards the edge of the universe and the beginning of time. Astronomers think that the oldest galaxies in the image formed less than a billion years after the Big Bang.

What Hubble Can't See

Although Hubble can see things billions of light-years away, it isn't much good for looking at things nearby. HST can't see things on Earth because it's moving too fast relative to the ground. It can't study the Sun because the Sun is too close and too bright. Although it can see large objects that are very far away, HST can't see small objects up close. For example, it could never see the flag that the astronauts left on the Moon.

Since Hubble's instruments are designed to look only at infrared, visible, and ultraviolet light, it can't observe radio waves, X rays, microwaves, or gamma rays. Other space telescopes such as the Chandra X-Ray Observatory are designed to look at those types of light.

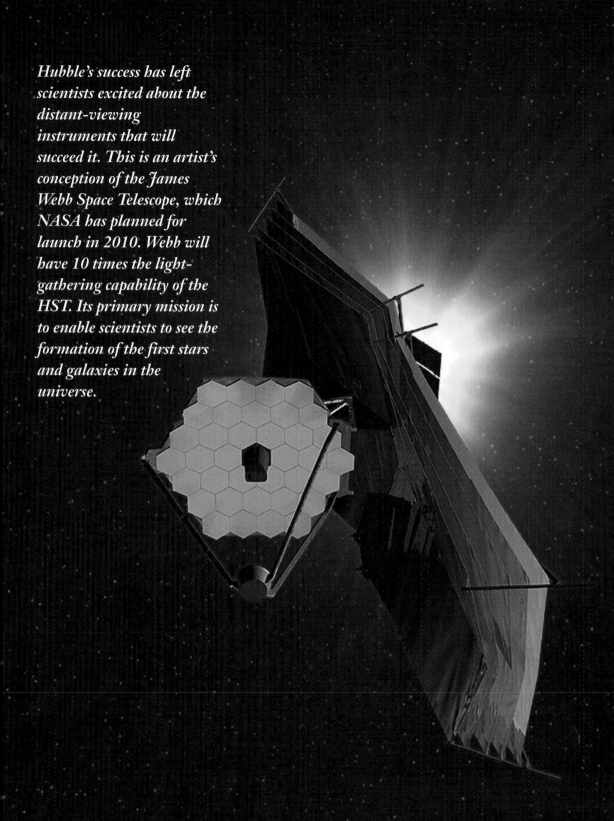

Hubble's success has left scientists excited about the distant-viewing instruments that will succeed it. This is an artist's conception of the James Webb Space Telescope, which NASA has planned for launch in 2010. Webb will have 10 times the light-gathering capability of the HST. Its primary mission is to enable scientists to see the formation of the first stars and galaxies in the universe.

Chapter Four

The Future

Originally, NASA planned to keep Hubble in orbit for fifteen years. It has been working so well, however, that they've decided to keep it up for another five years. The plan right now is for HST to retire in 2010. Astronauts will travel up in a space shuttle, bring HST into the shuttle's cargo bay, and carry it back to Earth.

What then? The data Hubble collected could keep scientists busy for many, many years. But scientists and engineers are never satisfied with what they have. When HST retires, it will be time to launch a new telescope, one that can collect more light and see farther away and farther back in time. The new telescope is called the James Webb Space Telescope (JWST), named after the man who was in charge of NASA during the Apollo Moon landings.

Unlike HST, JWST won't orbit Earth. Instead, it will orbit the Sun in a much darker and colder part of space nearly a million miles (1.5 million km) away. It will have a primary mirror six times the size of HST's and will have instruments that can detect infrared light that Hubble could never see. If everything goes as planned, JWST will be able to see objects that are one hundred times fainter than what Hubble can see. It will also be able to detect light form just a few million years after the Big Bang. NASA calls the James Webb Space Telescope "the First Light Machine."

JWST

The James Webb Space Telescope was originally known as the Next Generation Space Telescope.

HST

All together, over its twenty-year mission, the HST program will cost about $6 billion. This works out to about $300,000 for each 97-minute orbit.

Timeline

1608	The telescope is invented in Holland
1609	Italian astronomer Galileo Galilei uses a telescope to look at the Moon, planets, and stars
1923	Decades before the space age begins, rocket scientist Hermann Oberth publishes his idea for putting a telescope into orbit.
1924	American astronomer Edwin Hubble discovers that the Milky Way is not the only galaxy in the universe—the nearby Andromeda Nebula is also a galaxy
1929	Edwin Hubble discovers that the universe is expanding
1957	The Soviet Union launches the first artificial satellite *Sputnik 1* into space
1958	NASA is established
1962	*Ariel 1*, the first space telescope, goes into orbit to study ultraviolet and x-ray radiation from the Sun
1968	The United States launches *OAO-II*, an orbiting observatory. For 4½ years it observes the ultraviolet emissions of galaxies, stars, planets, and comets
1977	The U.S. Congress approves funding to put a space telescope in orbit
1981	The Space Telescope Science Institute (STScI) established
1983	The telescope named after American astronomer Edwin Powell Hubble
1986	The Hubble Space Telescope launch delayed because of the *Challenger* accident
1990	The Hubble Space Telescope put into orbit from the space shuttle *Discovery*
1993	The Servicing Mission 1: COSTAR optics installed to correct the lens problem on HST

1997	Servicing Mission 2
1999	Servicing Mission 3A
2002	Servicing Mission 3B
2004	Planned Servicing Mission 4
2010	Planned retirement of HST; launch of the James Webb Space Telescope

Glossary

astronomer—a scientists who studies outer space: what it's made of, how it has changed through time, and the forces that make it look and act the way it does

electromagnetic radiation—a form of energy that travels as waves at the speed of light (the fastest speed known); visible light, microwaves, and radio waves are a few of the forms of electromagnetic radiation

electromagnetic spectrum—the range of electromagnetic radiation, from gamma rays to radio waves

galaxy—a group of millions to billions of stars, held close to each other by gravity

HST—the abbreviation for the Hubble Space Telescope

interstellar matter—anything that exists in space between the stars, mostly dust and gas

mass—the amount of material something is made of; mass is usually measured in grams (g) or kilograms (kg); on Earth, one kg weighs about 2.2 pounds

massive—an adjective describing something with a lot of mass

nebula—a cloud of dust and gas between or around stars

optical telescope—a telescope that observes visible light (the light we can see with our eyes)

planet—a large spherical object that orbits a star

planetary nebula—a cloud of dust and gas that looks vaguely planet-shaped (planetary nebulae have nothing to do with planets)

radio telescope—a telescope that observes radio waves

red giant—a very big, red star that forms when a moderate-sized star grows larger near the end of its life (before it becomes a white dwarf)

red supergiant—a huge red star that forms when a massive star expands near the end of its life (before exploding catastrophically)

reflecting telescope—a telescope that collects and focuses light using a system of curved mirrors (the light reflects off the mirrors)

refracting telescope—a telescope that collects and focuses light using glass lenses (the light refracts through the lenses)

satellite—an object that orbits another object in space; the Moon is a natural satellite of Earth, and HST is an artificial satellite

solar system—a star and all the planets, asteroids, comets, and other materials orbiting it

spectrograph—a scientific instrument that separates light into its different colors, and then measures and records how much of each color there is in the spectrum

spectrum—the specific colors that a particular object emits or reflects; every object has a distinctive spectrum

supernova—a catastrophic explosion that occurs at the end of the life of a very massive star

telescope—an instrument that gathers light and focuses it, creating magnified images that allow the person using it to see things that are too small or too far away to see with his or her eyes

ultraviolet light—light with wavelengths slightly shorter than visible light

wavelength—the distance between one wave crest and the next; each form of electromagnetic radiation has a different wavelength; every color of visible light has a certain wavelength

white dwarf—an old, collapsed star in the process of dying

To Find Out More

This book is really just an introduction to the Hubble Space Telescope. There is a lot more to learn about the telescope, and much, much more to learn about astronomy and the objects that HST has helped scientists study. As with all books, articles, and webpages, be aware of who the authors are and when they published their work. Some sources are out-of-date or not very reliable.

Books

Petersen, Carolyn Collins, and John C. Brandt. *Hubble Vision: Further Adventures with the Hubble Space Telescope*, Cambridge, UK: Cambridge University Press, 1998.

Spangenburg, Ray and, Kit Moser. *The Hubble Space Telescope*, Danbury: Franklin Watts, 2002.

Spangenburg, Ray and Kit Moser. *Observing the Universe*, Danbury: Franklin Watts, 2003.

Mitton, Simon and Jacqueline. *The Young Oxford Book of Astronomy*, Oxford: Oxford University Press, 1995.

Websites

The best places to find reliable, up-to-date information about HST are the official HST and NASA websites.

The Hubble Project
ttp://hubble.gsfc.nasa.gov/

The Hubble Site
http://hubblesite.org

The Space Telescope Science Institute
http://www.stsci.edu/resources/

Where is Hubble Now?
http://hubble.gsfc.nasa.gov/hubble-operations/tracking.html

ESA's Space Telescope Site
http://hubble.esa.int/

James Webb Space Telescope
http://ngst.gsfc.nasa.gov/

Learn more about the images in this book. STScI has in-depth explanations of Hubble images on the web.
http://oposite.stsci.edu/pubinfo/PR

Amazing Space
http://amazing-space.stsci.edu.
Web-based interactive games and other activities

All about Orbital Telescopes
http://seds.lpl.arizona.edu/~spider/oaos/oaos.html

How Telescopes Work
http://howstuffworks.lycoszone.com/telescope.htm

How a Prism Works (interactive)
http://micromagnet.fsu.edu/primer/java/scienceopticsu/newton

Ask an Astronomer
http://curious.astro.cornell.edu/index.php

Top Astronomy Sites
http://www.oup.co.uk/oxed/children/yoes/sites/space/

Places to visit or write to for more information

These places have exhibits specifically about the Hubble Space Telescope.

The Space Telescope Science Institute
3700 San Martin Drive
Baltimore, MD 21201

Maryland Science Center
601 Light Street
Baltimore, MD 21230
(410) 685-5225
www.mdsci.org

National Air and Space Museum
7th and Independence Ave. SW
Washington, DC 20560
(202) 357-2700
www.nasm.si.edu

A Note on Sources

A subject like the Hubble Space Telescope is a little more difficult to write about than others because it contains a mixture of history and current events. Hubble has now been in space for more than a decade, but it is gathering new information every day. This means that all the books about Hubble are a bit out-of-date as soon as they're published. The sources I found most useful were the official websites of the HST (see *To Find Out More*). These sites have an enormous amount of information about the telescope's history and how it works. They also include loads of images and their explanations, and are up-to-date about everything that is going on with the telescope. Since my background is in planetary geology, not astronomy, I also had to learn a lot of basics about stars and galaxies. *The Young Oxford Book of Astronomy* by Simon and Jacqueline Mitton, which is written for young adults, was extremely useful. I also learned a lot from my husband, Richard Ash, and from Alex Storrs, who used to be a researcher at the Space Telescope Science Institute and is now a professor at Towson University. He spent an entire afternoon with me discussing his research and answering my questions. Finally, I was very fortunate to be able to tour the Space Telescope Science Institute and talk to a number of scientists who work with HST. Dorothy Fraquelli, Marc Postman, and Charlie Loomis were all very generous with their time.

Index

Numbers in *italics* indicate illustrations.

About the Author

Margaret W. Carruthers is the author of several science books for children, including *Pioneers of Geology: Discovering Earth's Secrets* and the *Young Oxford Encyclopedia of Science: Land, Sea, and Air*.

Margaret has a B.S. in natural resources from the University of the South in Sewanee, Tennessee, and an M.S. in geology from the University of Massachusetts, Amherst. For her thesis, she studied a group of mysterious channels and craters on the surface of Mars.

Before becoming a writer, Margaret worked as a geologist and educator at the American Museum of Natural History in New York City. Since leaving the museum, she has written and edited many books and articles, taught in a primary school in Oxford, England, and worked for the National Museum of Natural History in Washington, D.C.

Margaret and her husband, cosmochemist Richard Ash, now live in Baltimore, Maryland.